In Her Hands

Michelle Bouverie

First published 2025

Text copyright © Michelle Bouverie 2025
The moral right of the author has been asserted

All rights reserved. No part of this publication may be reproduced, stored in a retrieval system, or transmitted in any form or by any means, electronic, mechanical, photocopying, recording or otherwise, without the prior written permission of the publisher and copyright holder.

Cover illustration by Mahala Newland

A self published title
Designed and produced by Adala Publishing
www.adalapublishing.com.au

 A catalogue record for this book is available from the National Library of Australia

ISBN 978-0-6453485-5-2 (Print)
ISBN 978-0-6453485-6-9 (eBook)

For you, Jaine

My soul sister, my safe place, my dear friend.

For the love, laughter and friendship we shared.

May our Great Mother hold you, safely

In Her Hands x

Goddess

Flow like the River

Feel yourself

Disarm

Purpose

In the garden of my next life
If that is where I'll be
I'll return as a Willow
Or a Mountain Mahogany

I'll move with the wind
There'll be no break in my bend
And my roots
They will dive

Reach
And extend
Into the warmth and nurture
Our Mother Nature lends

My branches
Sovereign and proud
Will extend with belonging
To the service of shade

Where,
In daylight I'll be the relief
And by night

I'll be the wild

In which I was conceived

I'll just be there.

Being.

A tree.

Escapism

Wind

Colliding with the leaves

And the trees

Messy escapes through narrow features

Wind

Beating heavily at my door

Persistent in its erratic mood!

No patience in its wild pursuit!

Why, I wonder?

Angry

Whining wind

Why do you claw so violently

At my door?

I envisage our bodies

Colliding on the back step

Wind 1 Michelle None

Wind

Invisible chaos

Escapism at its finest

Conversations with the Mother

Daughter

It's just you and I here

No whispers or intrusions

Breathe out

So, I may breathe you in

Smell the scent of all that blooms

See the beauty in my flowing lines

Feel each heartbeat

Mine with yours

Yours with mine

Hear my whisper in the wind

Taste the freedom of birds in flight

You are held completely

There is no doubt

Awash your senses

With me, delightfully

Your love

Bears the fruit

Of my sanctuary

Create from your pain
Until you feel whole again

Tempered Masks

How the tempest winds

Beckon forth the mask of fear

Uprooting sharp, buried memories

Which should no longer reside here

How the rolling seas of sorrow

Pierce and decay this deepened burrow

For masks have hidden

Only for the time

That songbirds couldn't decipher the rhyme

How the passionate crumbling

Of the earth to its mist

A wholeness

To a nothing

To a something

To a kiss

Lips

The gateway to reflection and taste

The beating of the heart

Spaced not to waste

As the mask of never needing

Is adorned no more
The whispers of silk
And satin
Like residue of yesterday
Naked on the floor

Shadow Work

Spiraling

Down, down below

Where truth exists

In the darkness

Succumbing

To what makes me

Me

The path before,

The now, and

What may come

Here I am

Embodying the peasant!

My suffering

In rags

Bound by the snags of existence

Here I am

Small

Defeated

Meeting today

Alone

Afraid

Yet Still Rising

Time

Timidly you pass, most powerful muse
Yet bold in your intent
Tearing down the walls of fantasy and expectation

Our sorrow held in the time we borrow
As you whisper
In the swoon of moonlight breaking
That new moments shall appear tomorrow

How gentle is your hand which holds promise
From the first cries of birth
To the last breath of death, then
To vanish in presence beyond the realm of that last breath

Precious Time, we know that you are there
Inconspicuous
As we huddle
In the safety of attachment, plans and prayer

And the tick tock of the clock chimes in rhyme
As you drape yourself like gold across shoulders broad in struggle

Where hope is carried in your foresight
Yet the same collation of moments in your whisper
Is the harmony to our undoing

Time
You have lined many a chapter with kindness
As you linger entwined with the seasons
And dance!
Dance
As the gatekeeper
Welcoming our surrender

So that we may step forward more freely
Into the unknown.

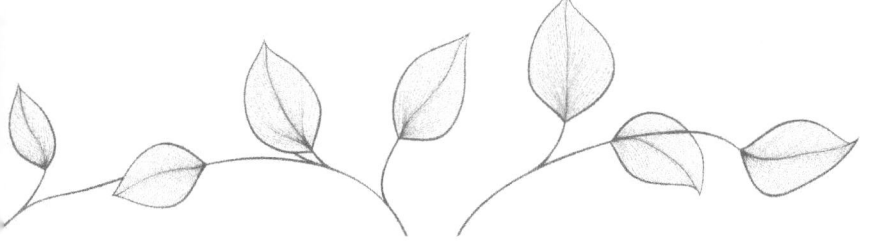

I am grateful for boundaries, books and long slow kisses

Lovers

Two lovers

Held in sensual embrace

Hearts open

With love the binding lace

Breath warm and so sweet to taste

Skin igniting with response

To the hunger in each touch

Raging silence

Burning with each clutch

Sensual energy

A rising affair

Flesh

Lips

Goosebumps

And ruffled, flowing hair

No moment too late

No moment too soon

Two Lovers embrace

Under the light of the New Moon.

Committed

I have loved you
And tasted the sweetness of those words
As I offered them to you.

I have loved you
And mended the breaks in my heart
With faith in love, the glue.

I have loved you
Reaching into the reserves of love
I held for me
To shine some light when your light needed rest.

I have loved you
When I have been my worst
And you have been your best.

I have loved you
Like a lark in serenade to the sun
I have loved you

And that is all there is.

Boundaries

Don't look for me in the moonlight
Don't look for me by the sun
Don't look beyond the vast copper fields
Where pain's inflicted, not undone

Don't look for me in the depth
Of the darkness which you feel
Don't look for me
When you cross the bridge
Between truth and identity

Don't pull me back to sadness
Don't pull be back to pain
Don't pull me back to the fingerprints
On another's heart, in pain

I know you're hungry for forgiveness
I know you're hungry for reprieve
But the peace you seek
When you're tender and meek
Is the burning you must face

I forgive you for these prickly gifts
You've left burrowed in my heart
No right or wrong entwines us
Healing begins at last.

The river of experience, love and connection
Flows abundantly, wide and full

Sit yourself by the river side
Allowing the water's edge to lap against your toes

Just Be.

The Queen & Her Crown

Did you see me

As I whispered my love's patience

Gently in your ear?

Did you see me

As I held your pain and your sorrow

Safely in my heart?

Did you see me

As your past in painful torment

Broke in,

To tear this love apart?

Did you see me

As I rose to the occasion

Time and time again?

Did you see me

As I fell to my knees

Exhausted

My heart in pieces

Love begging to be let in?

Did you see me

As I screamed my words in silence

For fear of your contempt?

Did you see me

As my thoughts became contorted

Seeking solace in a silent vent?

Did you see me

As you paved the path to confusion

Mystery

Your intent?

Did you see me

As I laid my depleted heart at your feet

Seeking acknowledgement?

Now I ask you,

Old Lover, Old Friend

In a seven-year evolving through time

Do you see me now?

As I breathe in nature's courage

Her pain mine, and mine hers spent!

And I rise to my feet

Where Self Love and I meet

And reposition my fucking crown!

As I rise to MY occasion

Releasing your lies and my regret!
Eradicating your pain from my heart
One of my greatest challenges yet!

So now my love,
I bid you Adieu
For within this newfound light I've found
Finally,

I SEE YOU!

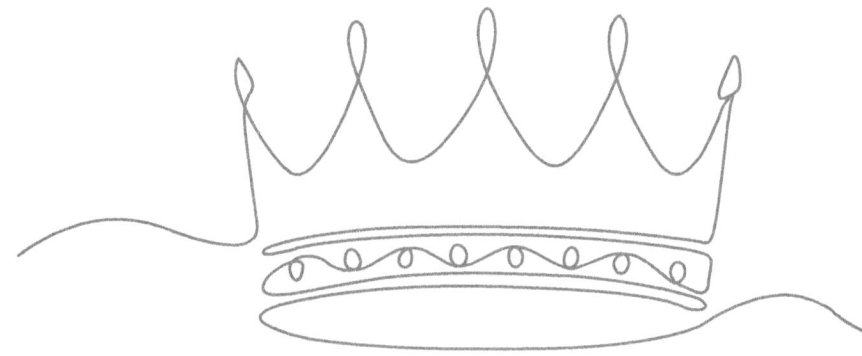

Grief

I build my life

Over a river of sadness

Where banks of survival

Keep it contained

I build a bridge

So I may walk across it

And feel only droplets

From rapids

At play

I build my house

Over a river of sadness

It runs

And washes my fears away

I build my dreams

Over a river of sadness

It generates hope

Where darkness once lay

I build my life

Over a river of sadness

It's always there

As a measure of grace

I build

And I cry

A river of sadness

Its depth breeds belonging

As the place it will stay

I build my courage

Over a river of sadness

To be whole

To be seen

To wash my shield away

I build my love

Over a river of sadness

For love is the current

Guiding its way

Layers

I peeled back a layer of control
And whispered 'I love you' as I did so
The eyes of time assessing me
Adventure in surrender
Harvesting fear in me

Another layer
I gently lifted
With consciousness
Attuning
To time's foreign whispers
The legacy of touch
Not offering support
I fell to my knees
As the teacher is taught

In the place where strength
Could no longer be felt
My curiosity exposing
All that time had dealt
Confusion and fear
And a calling for peace

The supportive hand of friendship
Guiding me deeper towards release

From the magic of the soul
I pushed through the layers of control
A crying child
A wounded daughter
A broken mother held
In the heart of a tempered lover

Surrounded by my shadows
In their darkness, seeking grace
I found my feet, in gust and wind
And looked each one in the face

The eye of consciousness held my gaze
A reveal of the journey that has been
As I opened my arms
And in a desperate cry
I surrendered
And saw
What was awakened to be seen

Sadness will arrive some days.

Let her.

With love, hold space for her too.

Feel her presence, and the wholeness she brings to each purposeful beat of your heart.

Forgiveness, The River

Lightly
We stepped
Along cobble stones
To the River

We breathed in her beauty
Where old, majestic relics
Held by shield of bark
Reached from her tender banks
Casting comfort in their shadow

The tears of time
In motion, constant
Lapping the shore
And gently reaching to our bones
As we lay our troubles
On her banks

Giving thanks

For all that had come
Then washed away with her current

So silent.

Self-Soothing

Be still oh bleeding heart, be still
For love so secretly tore apart
The deeper layers which you shared
Blinded by your tainted will.

Be calm oh weeping heart, be calm
Though cracks may seep with deepened sorrow
Find grace in the light which may appear
Expand with the energy, which breath brings to borrow.

Be light oh weary heart, be light
Find buoyancy in your beat
Remove the sadness, that weighs like darkness
Through your darkest night's sleep.

Take flight adventurous heart, take flight
Which direction is wrong,
and which is right?
Seek freedom from the judgement of life's rigid compass.

Soar, brazen heart! Soar!
Mother Nature provides glorious color to inspire

Each mountain an inspiration, so lift even higher!
Be Bold! Be Alive! Be Here! Be Now!
Each beat defines your own life's song.

Heal now, loving heart, heal
Invite pure light into every crevice
And where the memory of loss remains,
Breed new life from the inspiration of tomorrow.

The Unfuckening

The Unfuckening

Is the reach deep down inside

To find soot layered canyons

Gouged!

From the explosive shattering of your heart

Broken shards you carry

Disdained!

Dazed!

Naked in the winter mist

Questioning your reality.

The Unfuckening

Is the wretched uncovering of truth!

The Truth!

A kaleidoscope in which you seek your sanity!

Sanity revealed

Lifted

Gifted

It's the plot twist!

The Unfuckening
Is in the suffering sounds
Of the forgiveness you give
But the apology you never receive!
It's the silence.
The silence you sit inside
When you think all hope is lost.

The Unfuckening
Is the place,
Oh Yes, it's the place!
Where you find yourself
And lose yourself,
Over and over again!
Unfuck and unfuck yourself
Over and over again!
In the intuitive whispers
From deeper within.

The Unfuckening!
Now that's where living begins.

It's difficult to appreciate the light in its fullness

Without the shadows illuminating its glow

One cannot be, without the other.

The Polarity of Life

Poets Journey

I wrote a poem about pain
As the sharp knife edge
Of its presence guided my pen
Filling the landscape of my page
Until I felt peace again.

I wrote a poem about loss
And swam in her tides
Submerged in her waves I was.
A beautiful oasis arose
Calling me home
To take comfort, in the tears I had wept.

I wrote a poem about forgiveness
To embrace another's mistakes
As a mirror to my own
And to see
We are all
Just walking each other home.

Messages in the Night

In your slumber

Do you wake

To the stillness of your mind?

Do you fly there?

Do you try, there?

To make peace with what you find

In your slumber

Do you conjure

Manifest

And read the signs?

Do you wake there?

Do you shake there?

To the magical Divine

Venus Rising

Heart lifting to the sun
Soul calling to the moon
Love, my anchor to this earth
Love, my nurturing cocoon
Guide me Mother Earth
No more shackles
No more plight
Guide me, radiant Mother
Back to the radiance of your light.

I am unafraid to shine

To crumble

To rage

I am unafraid

The whispers of the caterpillar becoming a butterfly

Brave

There lays the seed,
Deep within the soil of the Great Mother
Encased in the dense darkness,
And Brave in trusting the rain to fall.

In the leap of faith
Of the baby bird from its Mother
Is newborn courage expanding as wings
And held by the silence of instinct in its hover
With heartbeat lifting bravery
Into the beauty of Spring.

There beneath the softness
Of once a broken-hearted Mother
Is the whisper of bravery inviting
Courage through the door

Each moment offering,
Another moment to discover
The magic in the symphony
Of bravery being born.

Reflection

I looked in the mirror at my reflection
My naked body exposing
Flesh and feelings

I opened my mouth
And whispered 'I love you'
Green eyes connecting with green eyes

A tear released.

I knew my love was true.

Meet yourself in the small place, friend

Meet yourself in the small place, friend
Go there, and meet away the
Tight twists of nervosity holding you small.
Stay there. Feel there.
Take the punches, and the crunches
Breathe.
The storm will pass,
Wisdom will meet you there
Inviting you to grow.

Meet yourself in the lonely place, friend
Go there, and meet away
Echo's cast by empty rooms, lonely moons.
Stay there. Feel there.
Draw meaning from the hollow
Breathe.
Hear the whispers beneath the echo
Courage will meet you there,
Inviting you to grow.

Meet yourself where you are, friend

Go there, and meet away

Your doubts, your fears and the labels which you wear.

Become the friend you always needed,

The lover you always believed in

Be kind as you go there, friend

Love will meet you there,

Inviting you to grow.

Love is love is love

And sometimes love is pain,

Discomfort,

And a rapid disheveling of what we think we know

So that we may find freedom to grow

Wild Mistress

Grief is a wild mistress
She is bondage, she is play
She is the sweet sensuality of love making
Inviting you to stay.

She is Kali. She is Ganesh.
She. Is. Powerful!

Feel Her!
Allow her to be so.

Moon Medicine

Come sit, she said

Step outside of your head

Breathe me in

It's free

Share your sorrows

With me

I am yours

Always here

There is nothing

To fear

Come sit

Theres always room

Under the light

Of the highest moon

We are both

Of salt, and tides

No cage here

No need to hide

Come sit

I'm here with you

Under the light

Of the highest moon

Close your eyes

Do you see?

This love is you

This love is me

Come sit

I'm here with you

Under the light

Of this radiant moon.

Pocket of Joy

War erupted across the seas that night
Deep cries of sorrow filled the air
Children screamed for their mothers
Yet no one seemed to hear
Buildings fell like dominoes
a match of 'Who Would Win!'
But no one cared for the children
Whose lives were in suffering
Many hands rummaged through wreckage
Of homes once filled with joy
Reaching for just one heartbeat
Life so easily destroyed
War erupted across the seas that night
Medics cried for relief
Yet no one could hear the children
Who suffered
hungry and weak.

The sun soon arose to rubble
Light shone through the debris
No more bombs erupted

A stillness brought reprieve
Although the cries were present
In distance, and from fear
A child emerged dust covered
To see his father near
His father's face was desperate
Tears flowing for his boy
Within the carnage of suffering
There, was a pocket of joy!
One hand held within the other
They walked the solemn ground
If only for a moment

Joy lived, in being found.

The possibilities become endless as time persists,

and the awakening of our internal summer is upon us.

Pillow Talk

Before I lay my head down to rest
The silver linings I hold
In acknowledgement
Where mistakes often sit
In darkened remiss
And the soft glow of sunrise
Peaks, through the morning mist

Before I venture into my dreams
I ask to be guided safely on my way
Where dreams in twilight unfold in color
And the puzzle pieces lift
With the lightness of butterfly wings
To be pieced back together with not a sign
But an ease in the solving of their ways

Before I begin again tomorrow
I retreat to the humbling
Lessons of the day
And call on my guides
To lay in comfort
By my side

To keep me safe
Should mischief come to play

And when the dawn of a new day is upon me
With the Great Mother's courage
Thickened in dew
I rise with a knowing
A deep, seeded knowing that

Yesterday
Is but a memory
Tomorrow
Too far to see
And right here in this moment
Is exactly where I'm meant to be.

Human

Allow yourself

To feel defeated

Allow the ache

To rise

Allow yourself

The pain of loss

There's no need to justify

Allow yourself

The discomfort

Allow yourself

The despair

Feeling and healing my friend

Are a sovereign pair

Allow yourself the tears

The aches, the breaks

The blues!

Allow yourself to be human

I'm here,

Being human too!

I Am Love

I wait for him
Like the storm clouds above
Waiting to explode
With their love.

I call out to him,
'Let me be the rain!'

I am love.

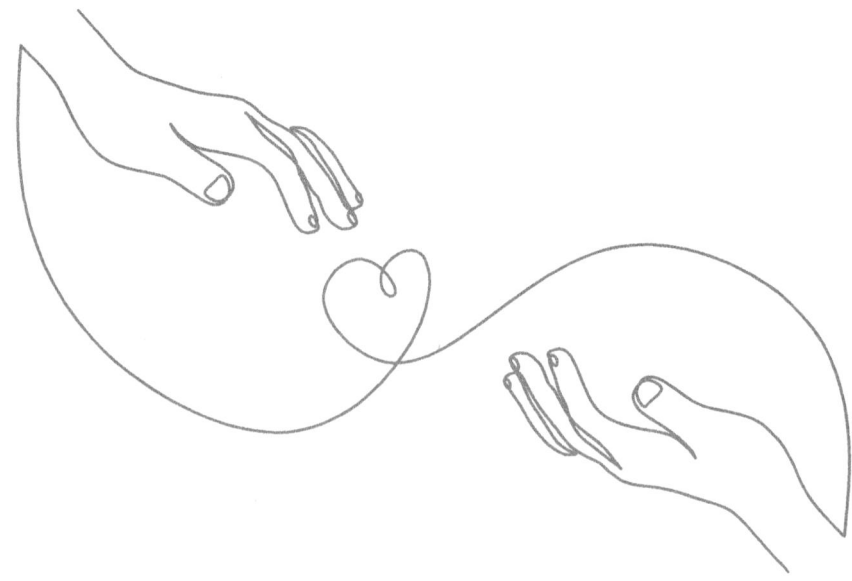

What a privilege it is

to swim in the joy of connection and solitude

to alchemize pain into beauty

to embrace this offering of life at my feet

I am grateful.

When it hurts

Don't wait!
Travel to the edge of reason
To discover the magic of you
Take the scenic route
Speak kindly,
Clutching the hand of forgiveness
Allow her to lead you to freedom
Kiss with wanting passion
Make love
Touch with curious desire
Breathe in the salty air.

Dance

Dance like it hurts to stand still!

To Contemplate

It was on the lush, green grass
Where I lay,
Contemplating
The movements of the day.
The crisp, comforting breeze
Soothed the dance of my thoughts
Inviting each eyelid to gently close,
As my fingertips discovered
The cool sensation of soil.

Contemplating
The moments uniting
With the slow, steady journey of the clouds
Mirroring the endless promise
Of time always passing.

And as I lay
Contemplating
The movements of the day
I felt the steady earth beneath me,
Holding me

Reminding me to stay with purpose,

To ground

For within this stillness,

The answers are found.

Hold Her Close

Do not be afraid

To bring her ear

Close,

To your chest.

Feel her safety

In the rhythm

Of your beating heart

In rest.

Hold her close

To the sound

Of your courage

Brewed in test.

For today

And tomorrow

For life, and all the rest.

Hold her smile

In your mind

To replay

When she forgets.

Lift her spirit

Ignite her fire

She'll return to you

Reset.

Hold her close

In your love

May it be

The greatest yet.

To let go

To arrive

In love's safe nest.

Inhale

Pause

Exhale

Pause

Consciously moving

Closer to yourself

Sunbeam

If I were a sunbeam

I'd reach so close to the lining of your thoughts

No grey or encumbered shadow would stay

I'd wait for love's invitation to beam right in

And on the stage of eternity

There would be

The dance of your magic

And serenity at play.

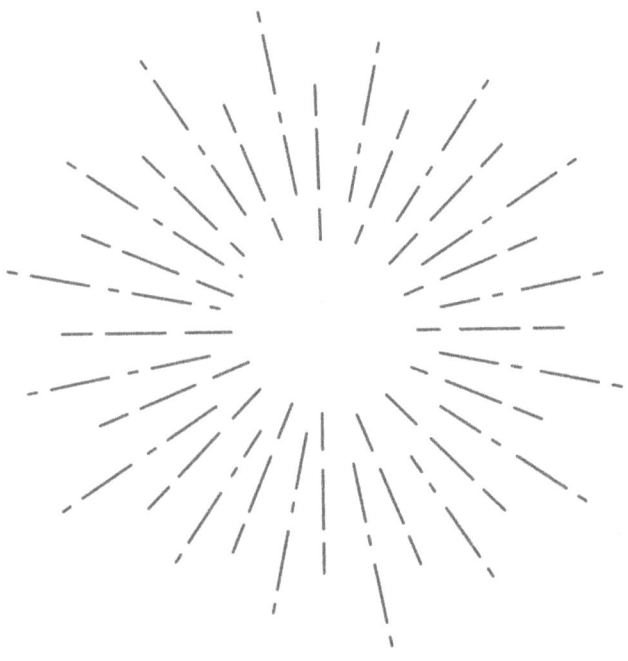

Sanctuary

In the lush expanse

Of landscape

Spread,

Where trees

Reach and sway,

By wind caressed.

Beneath skies

Adorned,

With a crystallized flow

Behold the sanctuary

Of beauty

Mother Nature in flow.

Soften to her sounds,

Taste the

Richness of her fruit,

Expand your senses

Let breath

Be the root,

To all that she offers

Dancing seasons

In bloom.

Find comfort
And safety
Under the light
Of her moon.

Rapture in Venus

May time keep you wild

In the rapture of space

May no mould

Or encumbrance

Tarnish the light in your face

May this dance in the moonlight

Ignite adventure through taste

May time keep you wild

Venus

Held

And embraced.

Love Is

Love is

The Muse

To which all

Undoing

And

Becoming

Heed to

And

Reach toward

Gentler

Than a whisper

More ferocious

Than the storm

Humbler than

A beggar

Intimate

Beyond passion

As a witness

To the dawn

Love is

The Honey

And the Nectar

And the Bee

The fruit of inspiration

Connecting

You and Me

The voyeuristic moon was bright that night, illuminating
    the shadows below
of those who were brave enough to be seen.

www.ingramcontent.com/pod-product-compliance
Lightning Source LLC
Chambersburg PA
CBHW062043290426
44109CB00026B/2715